CW01334572

METHUEN PAIRED READING STORYBOOKS

Scribble Sam

Bill Gillham

Illustrated by Gerald Rose

Methuen Children's Books

Sam can't read and write and draw.

But he can scribble.

He scribbles everywhere.

On the wall . . .

and on the floor.

Down the stairs . . .

and up the hall.

Run!

Sometimes he even scribbles on himself!

His mum bathed him and
put his chalks away.

'No more scribbling, Sam,' she said.

Next day Sam was missing.

'I've lost my little boy,' said his mum. 'He scribbles.'

Out of the gate and down the road was one long scribble.

'Follow that scribble!' they shouted.

Round the corner . . .

through the supermarket . . .

over a baby's pram.

And there was Sam,
scribbling away.

'Sam,' said his mum, 'don't you ever go scribbling again.'

This is Sam back home.
Is he scribbling?

Oh, no – Sam doesn't scribble any more.

How to pair read

1 Sit the child next to you, so that you can both see the book.

2 Tell the child you are *both* going to read the story *at the same time*. To begin with the child will be hesitant: adjust your speed so that you are reading almost simultaneously, *pointing to the words* as you go.

3 If the child makes a mistake, repeat the correct word but *keep going* so that fluency is maintained.

4 Gradually increase your speed once you and the child are reading together.

5 As the child becomes more confident, lower your voice and, progressively, try dropping out altogether.

6 If the child stumbles or gets stuck, give the correct word and continue 'pair-reading' to support fluency, dropping out again quite quickly.

7 Read the story *right through* once a day but not more than twice, so that it stays fresh.

8 After about 5-8 readings the child will usually be reading the book independently.

In its original form paired reading was first devised by Roger Morgan and Elizabeth Lyon, and described in a paper published in the Journal of Child Psychology and Psychiatry (1979).

First published in Great Britain in 1987
by Methuen Children's Books Ltd, 11 New Fetter Lane, London EC4P 4EE
Text copyright © 1987 Bill Gillham.
Illustrations copyright © 1987 Gerald Rose
Printed in Great Britain ISBN 0 416 63830 9